T0065570

A MINI MINSTREL'S
MIND

A MINI MINSTREL'S MIND

MANNAT RAO

PARTRIDGE

Print information available on the last page.

To order additional copies of this book, contact
Partridge India
000 800 10062 62
orders.india@partridgepublishing.com

www.partridgepublishing.com/india

contents

friendship

•

i can't tell you what friendship is
i can't make you understand this

it is literally the connection of broken souls
when broken
the heart bleeds with holes

i love you
i need you
i encourage you
i respect you

but not in vain
for you do too

i will trust you forever
no matter
whether we are far or together
you help me when i fall
you are the best of all

•

literature

•

from a chapter in class,
to a novel on the grass
we carry literature everywhere
in our books, in our hearts

whether Jane Eyre cries
or Dorian Grey pries
we feel what they feel
we see what they see

a gentle breeze when you're upset
a soft caress when things aren't set
a therapy of its own kind
getting us lost in the seas of our minds

smartly written, artistically insightful
literature, is of that, full
whatever the form
poetry, prose or drama
it remains a triumphant enigma

•

a silent cry

•

from over the green mountains
from under the sparkling stream
you can hear it everywhere
the echo of nature's scream

on barren land
tree stumps stand
littered across the earth
the picture of hypocrisy
as we cry when falls our hearth

the ice caps melting
the rain is pelting
and taking everything in its way
we have the nerve to cry
and to sob and to pry
when our resolve to destroy does not sway

lakes are murky
or every empty
and news segments fail to impress
but, when the water hits, oh, dear God!
you should see their dresses of tears

why so greedy, i ask you?
why this hunger, i implore

what was lacking in earth's leniency
that you went ahead and stole?

animals on the road
are lost with no direction
meaningless and unwanted
after an age of perfection

there's still time, i say
there's still time, i pray
for redemption is an art
you'll find it; look within your heart

so help me help you
help me save you
do you really think
i need to say more?

nature is a priceless gift of God
beware i say, taking largesse for granted
often leaves you tainted

•

memory

•

like the photos you clicked
like the flowers you picked
like the smiles you gave
in abundance and in rave

like the scorching sun above
inescapable, yet dazzling
like the pouring rain that day
musical, yet overbearing

like those rich shades of yellow
in the trees, in your hands
like the purple scarf you gave me
shabby in its strands

like the cold that followed
eerie and disturbed
like the silence that lingered
uneasy and perturbed

like the storm of the night
raging and fierce
like the clap of startling thunder
perilous and immersed

like the sky sheathed in grey
with that kick of bitterness
like the inevitable ending
sweet in its impending sourness

like the jacket i now fold
yours to say, but mine to keep
like the bag you now pack
final and discreet

like the echo of the door
slamming and whipping
like the sound of me sinking to the floor
and bursting in uncontrollable sobbing

like the letter months after
surprising and confusing
like the hearts that skips a beat
hoping for understanding

like the rip that followed
and the eagerness of a child
and like the disappearance of a rainbow
sudden before mild

like the way i ran
and like the way you sprinted
i, in joy
and you in elation untied

and like the embrace that followed
and the kisses borrowed
and despite it all
we were complete yet again

it's funny how the fates planned our loom
who knew that the storm
would be followed by a bloom?
and as you twine our fingers together
caressing as if holding a feather
i beam in the beauty of this little eternity
an age that ended
led to a fidelity

and as you brush the hair out of my eyes
i smile for i know, this will last our life

like the smiles you gave
in abundance and in rave

like the smiles you gave
in abundance and in rave

•

misery

•

the heart is clenched by
a bottomless well
pain echoes through
like a resounding bell

tear ducts, tireless
stop, no more
my eyes burn from
the pain you bore

shivering, trembling
hands are shaking
i reach up and swipe away
but it is pointless
for i have just opened
another trail of tears, here to stay

oh, pity me, pity me
i'm used to seeing
you through a film of tears

lips that wobble
knees that quake
is what you leave
in your wake

you smile, oblivious
eyes with glitter
are unaware in their bliss

of the pain, the suffering
the never ending misery
you have left me
ailing with

•

first love

•

the butterflies unrelenting erupt
in the pit of my stomach, they disrupt
a peace i'd worked hard to gain
a normalcy that's hard to attain

your eyes, sparkling smile
as if in knowing the length of this crime
i have committed by looking at you
my life changing from grey to blue

sinful lips pull up to smirk
realizing his effect and filled with mirth
a flash of brilliant white teeth
a mischievous smile, and a devilish gleam

i breathe in shakily, dazed
when you start your way to me in laze
i rake my eyes through your face
noting a dimple and a break
in your forehead as you shake our hands
relishing the sinewy muscles that stand

eyes that meet, lips that fight
against the smile that threatens to light
again a joke in sarcasm is cracked
ridiculing others to make her laugh

to hear the tinkling peal of bells
to watch the eyes that threaten to spill

they talk and talk and talk & talk
his jacket on her shoulders as they walk
the instinct to smile overwhelming
the urge to blush never ending

reaching the gate, i glare at it
wishing it to disappear, for a minute more late
turning towards her, i grin, soft
as i watch her nose turn pink with frost

she brushes away the strands let loose
stubborn, they push back and choose
a path for him that leaves him breathless

i step forward and tuck it back
enjoying her hitching breath as i touch her tress
lingering there, near her warmth
resisting the urge to kiss and caress
the waves of chocolate that frame her face

a strand caught at the edge of her
deliciously smart mouth
she shivers in delight, our eyes unblinking
pleading to stay, my hands are near begging

they bid goodbye and she walks in
but her steps are hesitant, her walk alien
"what is this weird pull", wonders she
" – that's holding me back and drawing me in?"

and at her door she turns
big doe eyes that yearn
to run back and never leave
to hug and kiss and smile and feel

in framed eyes, chocolate flashes
his heart stops and his breath catches
and then and there, they make a promise
to let this not be the last of their bliss
his hand raises, confirming his conviction
eyes twinkling with determination
she smiles brightly, satisfied
hesitant still, she goes inside

and somewhere between the both of them
him walking down the street,
her sitting on the sheets
their faces alight with a bright smile
at what has just unconsciously begun

•

sundered

·

are you just as lost
in the labyrinth in which i bow?

with no way out
and no way in
i've locked up my self
deep, deep within

the car light flashes
clashing with blue
your streaked hair creates
a silhouette around you

i wave until i can no longer
see you any more
and fight the urge to run back
sob for forgiveness, torn

and i'd have fared better then
being a wimp and maybe a coward
than drenching this poor pillow
with tears that run rampant

it rings with finality
tearing through my soul
leaving behind a wide gaping hole

no falter in your steps
no last look back
you carry on in your path
oblivious to the breathing i lack

i try not to linger
and to ponder and to render
myself irreparable by this strange sense of doom
you've left behind
eerie in its gloom

unpacking is torture
settling, a tragedy
and that picture of you and me?
is a rock too heavy

where are you now?
what are you now?
are you just as lost
in the labyrinth in which i bow?

where are you now?
what are you now?
are you just as lost
in the labyrinth in which i bow?

•

paris – that was

•

a scream that goes unheard
drowned out by thousands of others
lights flash, the fluorescent bright
rivers of red are drawn in the night

a fire forgotten burns in the corner
quietly crackling as if a stealthy hunter
it reminds me of our predicament
dark & pressing like a pending ailment

a blast distant goes off again
a home, a street, a family in pain
it's funny how i don't even flinch
numb from the usual, it doesn't even pinch

another cloud forms
of angry reds and raging orange
sparks and flickers, torn
contrast with the cobalt range

that same cloud blocks the stars
like the blood, mixed and lost
in the searing tar
a baby wails and cries and whimpers
who is it now?
a brother, a sister or a mother?

the building tall is silent in horror
speechless & aching
at the world of terror
a scream there
an eruption here
why does no one stop
and ask me how i bear?

the raging sirens
the endless bodies
a mother there
holding a tiny, limp body?

i'd not answer still
afraid to cry
when reminiscing the glory
the glory of that time

when laughs and songs could be heard
and the sun was free of clouds, undeterred
when the same mother would rock her child
marveling at his perfection soft & mild?

and then i'd ask you
dreading your answer
will no one ask me how i feel?

will no child make a tower of cards?
replicating me beyond the tar?
and giggle & clap when it falls
then make it again persevering hard?

will no one ask me how i feel?
and no one stop to look at me?
and gaze at me in awe again
to remember the glory
the glory of the Paris of yesterday

•

fireworks – 9 to 12

•

as the clock strikes 9
as the clock strikes 10
a look through the crowd
in success, in vain

people smile & wave in cheer
but my smile's faint
and lost & quaint

love is radiant
and endless & raging
and yet here i am
alone & aching

lanterns here, candles there
in tons & miles
our laughter will weigh

your words were sweet
but pending still
a whisper broken
echoes down the hill

you'd smiled & kissed
my cheek in soft
a warm summer breeze
in a wintry frost

and closed my eyes
and leaned in close
you whispered in my ear
and i blushed like a rose
"say fireworks if you like it"
and so i did
when your lips warm landed
on my frozen ones
when you held me tightly
and showered me in your love

and for all that love
i'm standing here alone
my lips are cold
and the whispers now torn

you're life, you're death
you're all that's in between
you're pain, you're love
you were mine to keep

you smiled, you laughed
and set the room aglow
you held, you kissed
creating fire in the snow

as the clock strikes 11
as the clock strikes 12
screams erupt & fireworks rave
a year later, not much has changed
lest you warmed me before
and now i'm a victim to the hail.

but, a warm breeze comes
caresses and goes
like a tender kiss
like the ones you used to give
and i look up at the stars
glittering in white
and blinking as if lazy
the memory's faint, but never hazy.

fireworks, then
fireworks, now
fireworks, forever, baby

fireworks, then
fireworks, now
fireworks, forever, baby

•

hello, december

•

mittens on, woolens out
puffs of air
in front of me are found
white frost lines the grass
hiding the green in a translucent glass

cocoa in my hand
socks on my feet
still i shiver
and grin in humble defeat

the mountains are shrouded
and murky & clouded
the thick fogs yet to dissipate
by the sun that's late to our gate

i look down at my fingers
at the icy blue i frown
hello, December
where did you come from?

but, until yesterday
the sun still shined
the birds still chirped
the flowers still smiled

don't get me wrong
i love the pretty snow
but i do miss the trees
of blooming greens despite no sow

but, why, oh, time?
are you so fast
couldn't you let April
a little longer last?

the lessons still new
redeeming still in hue
an abundance of chances
to correct the wronged tangents

the guides still apprehensive
in judging they were pensive
their eyes still soft
and not frozen with frost

•

eternal love

•

a field split with yellow
or a meadow green
white lands that stretch
or a river under the moon's sheen

sprinkled & scattered
thrown and studded
the blue with the white
that flaunts itself at night

or the white clouds
against a pale blue
white huffs of air
in different shapes or hues

a ray filtered, perhaps?
through leaves & branches
that falls and shines
finding perfection in mishaps

the soft sunset, then
in shades of orange
and types of pinks
or maybe the sunrise
rising through darkness
and shining like love

"a mother with her child", he says
marveling at his perfection in kind
"no, young love", they say
not like the dove, but like the swan they say

"first snow", she says
with even evil dressed in white
"rain after summer", they tell me
when earth is released from heat that simmers

"a groom in love", she insists
when his bride walks down the aisle
as the love shimmers & gleams
in his doting, adoring eyes

hot cocoa and a fire
that don't ever tire
pendants for two
and cold kisses shared through snow

if i asked what of beauty
your friends would tell me that
wistful and smiling
laughing and giggling
they'd relate their tales

they're pretty & nice
i'll grant them that
but nothing can ever beat
your shining blue orbs
filling me with glee

and your bubbling laughter
and the tilt of your brown head
and the freckles on your nose
or when your cheeks turn red

or your gleaming white smile
and when you hum a song
or brush back chocolate from your face
or gaze at me for too long

when you dance through the yellow field
when you smile at the meadow green
when you dip a toe in the glittering river
or beam at a white land
mingling with teal

when you lay back in the grass
with your hands behind your head
and stare at the starry sky
donned in a cape of dark blue lead

when you look up slightly
with a tilt of your chin
and ponder over what they resemble
a heart or a shin

when you sit at the counter
swinging your legs in glee
and when a gleaming ray hits your face
and when it caresses your face like a breeze

when you climb to the roof & fold your legs
and tuck your chin
and hum a gig
as the sun slowly bids you goodbye
you smile & sway in the beauty unconfined

when you wake me up
through slaps & nudges
the stars in your eyes
shining through the morning dawn

and point outside
as the sun ceases to hide
and crawls up slowly
spreading around like dust

when you beam at me
from under the snow
and laugh and giggle
in tones so low
your cheeks are flushed
your lips are frozen
but you kiss me still
as the white touches a dozen

and so i realize, and marvel and surmise
beauty isn't inanimate
or a thing or a serenade
beauty is appeal
beauty is love

now i'm given forlorn sympathy
and tears & tragedies
they pat my head
and shake their own
'poor guy, he's lost his love'

what's lost, i wonder?
you're right here
body, soul & heart are near
so why do they say sorry?
everything's fine, why the tears?

and once they leave
i glance up and shudder
and find you staring at me
in wonder

those same blue oceans
draw me in
hold me close
and keep me hidden

you're as beautiful as ever
flawless & without an error
i walk up close
and you hold my hand
those blue eyes are now
misty & shackled

you bring up my hand
and keep reaching up
until i'm touching
your smooth, soft scalp

you question me in quiet
begging & despaired
and then it hits me;
you thought i'd leave you unrepaired

i shake my head in anger
and hold you in my hands
and kiss you on the crown
devoid of chocolate strands

"beautiful", i whisper
and you recoil in shock
hesitant with joy
you sob to me "why?"

i smile at you gently
and kiss away your tears
beauty is love
beauty is eternal, dear!

•

twin souls

•

the blossoming rose
blooming through winter
the warm summer breeze
fragrance reaching my nose

whispers in secrecy
over tea are exchanged
and it's left untouched
in conversation inane

in pajamas and tops
through ice cream we talk
pillow fights & insomnia
through eyes that threaten to drop

hand in hand
we tromp through the snow
laughing at the footprints
dragging you in tow

you slip & fall
your face is shocked
i stare at you
then burst in laughter booming tall
and fall down, too
our hands are blue

for it's not just the mud
it's life we fell in
first you, then me in a huff

no knocking required where you're concerned
simply walk in, and announce "i'm home"
travelling miles to meet with you
then falling on the bed
and snoring through drool

your mother will find us
cuddling in sighs
entwined together
through dark & light

the jokes i crack
are hard do get
yet still you laugh
louder than the rest

we fight & curse
but live in verse
it's over, before we know it
and we're hugging in earnest

we live off of humour
and off laughter and off
private jokes that we grin at
booming with laughter
while others just sat

and then when at my worst i am
you'll hug me tight and coo in the light of the lamp
and wipe my tears hot & wet
my sweet, sweet friend
you're my comfort of years of pain

•

leave me alone

•

the notes are high, and still i reach
the rhythm is fast, and still i preach
old English or prose, i pull it off
i write and pour my emotions, lost

yes, the papers are filled with red
yes, maths and science go above my head

but i'm only human
and imperfect as i am
could you not overlook?
and forgive
and loosen?
the snare that's fastened around
my neck
the guilt that with years only gets decked

i know i am not ideal
or picturesque
on unreal
but, the ones who are
fair and far
are human, too
with me at par

so, why still, am i compared?
is individuality in this world so of late?

who said i have to study
to be respected?
you, me or society gets to make that gate?

so, yes, the paper's filled with red
yes, maths and science go above my head

but what happened to 'everyone's unique'?
and why are you killing,
killing that in me?

•

the perfect love

•

what keeps you up late at night
turning restless like a bird in flight
it causes your tummy to turn to mush
it plays your heart; tug & push

it makes you realize what they mean
when they say, 'my heart skipped a beat'
cause' when he saunters by lazily
your heart goes wild crazily

an oblivious step closer when he takes
your breath starts to hitch, and your knees shake
flowers suddenly mean much more
songs are hummed that you used to ignore

day dreaming is a constant chore
of beaches and roses and rings and shores
parents worry – "what has her smiling?
in a room all alone, brightly so?"

it takes some time but he soon realizes
a flash of brown follows him, tireless
but when he looks back to check;
she smiles at a baby, coos and pecks

he watches entranced
his stomach starts to dance
and his hands are sheathed in sweat
oh, dear heart; why do you react now so
when not ever before?

he blinks, frantic
eager to commit
all of her to memory
the shining hair
the smiling teeth
and the eyes that make him wobbly

and again it starts
the game of the hearts
when walking in the market
he peers closely
and thinks hard
which would she prefer; ring or locket?

then shaking his head
he'll scold himself
'fool, do you even know her name?'
'maybe not', he allows it so
'but i plan on making that change'

and when he smiles through his eyes
and leaves that stubble unshaven
your heart clenches at his rugged appearance
your teeth chatter at the goosebumps alien

"why", you wonder, "is he so kind?"
hadn't you seen enough to bind?
that feeling you get when you see
him crouching by a kid, hands on knees

oh, why, oh, why, does he approach you now?
has he caught you failing
at sneaking that glance?
your heart runs cold, your eyes are wide
the fear of rejection painfully ripe

you'd rather love him from far, you realize
than have him close and have to face the demise
of all the dreams you knit and wove
the silly fantasies he instantly invokes

but his husky voice does not snap
or blame or accuse or raise a suspicious glance
instead he takes you by surprise
and falls into a pattern
of conversation nice

"i'm talking to her!", he crows in his mind
singing and dancing and rejoicing in delight
oh, finally, finally, he has a chance
of holding her close and touching her strands

and as she smiles
his life flashes before his eyes
the nights spent praying
the days spent dreaming

of feeling inexplicable emotions
towards a teddy bear he saw her holding
of smiles and glances
others were exchanging
of standing in stores
trying to pick chocolates
of that burn of jealousy
when to others she was talking

of wanting to faint
when she flipped her hair
and of wanting to die
when she rolled her eyes

roses or lilacs remains the question
why does it feel
as if John Legend has you in detention?

why does she occupy your slot for dreams
messing with your heart; and now your sleep?
why do they say, "butterflies"?
when it's actually a zoo, crazy & wild?

you want to ask her:
'do you play guitar?
if not, then how are you so good with my mind?
forget my mind, you affect health, too!
where's a cardio surgeon when you need him so?
doctor, doctor help me please
my heart is erratic
is it supposed to skip a beat?'
why does she have to walk so gracefully
you feel as if your heart is what
she treads on peacefully

great, could it hurt some more?
couldn't she have just left your breath for sure?
but no, she takes that away, too
stealing it when she walks dressed in blue.

when, oh, when, did you become so cheesy?
why else would you be reading romances queasy?
why, oh, why, does marriage on a beach sound great;
a whole 18 years too late?

your room filled with soft toys
disturbs your parents
"should we check for fever or call an ambulance?
cause' last i checked he smiles so bright
only when he got those shoes, new and white"

you blink wildly
eyes focusing again
on the girl in front
and the beauty you might attain

you grin widely
ecstatic to think
that months of yearning might
actually bring some light

she blinks, startled
at the smile so bright
and ever so slightly
starts to smile

and as one, they both think
in their minds and their hearts
that burst with feels

simmer down, love, simmer down
caution to fall still remains
and on the package on which we'll sign
it'll say clear and bright

"lies inside a world of love
of pain and laughter like a grey streaked dove
beware, beware! there's a way to go about it
slowly, then all at once
slowly, then all at once"

•

identity

•

profession and name
of isolation or fame
an address of the suburbs
or a house in ruins

they say we're all different
in what way, though;
by essence or by the greetings lent?

is it open talents;
or hidden passions?
or maybe interests unattended
that burn to their own destruction

is it outside beauty?
dazzling & impressing;
or inner qualities?
subdued yet attracting

or may be society defines
our tranquilities & us
are you a woman who's undermined?
or a man; a picture of strength that's just?

what is it, then, that we identify ourselves with?
what do you want to be known by?
is it your appearance; fat or lithe?
or our hearts; pure and shy?

and yet still when we are asked
"who are you, stranger?"
we reply with our names
a fact that makes me wonder

why, that's your name
not your identity
they're your parents
not an infinite entity

you are who you are
for your loves & your passions
for the flickers of heat
that make up your reason

you are the fire behind your eyes
that smoulders while you're still
you are what you are alone
and not when you fall & tilt

and so it is said
the jury has stood
and the decision is read
the verdict is out
and is shouted clear & loud

you are what defines you
what together forms you
a mere name, a flimsy profession
can never contain you.

•

tavi

•

in the land like heaven
there flows a sparkling stream
singing and dancing
glinting under the sun's gleam

racing beside the green
and sprawling chinar trees
she is named, Tavi
the river that's as sacred as it's holy

but in sweet, sweet spring
she takes a different route
to visit the blossoming tree
standing tall & proud

through the different seasons
he moves back & forth
first a pink, then a white
like a raw, blunt frost

today, though the river wished
her passage could just pause
to gaze in wonder at the tree
at the yellow replacing the rose

the bright, bright sun
had lit the tree aglow
shiny yellow flowers
kissed the singing river's shore

the river sighed in longing
and bid the tree goodbye
"i'll be back soon", she said
" – to watch you light afire"

•

the Child of the Night

•

light, they say
is radiant beyond measure
washing the world in golden
like a glittering priceless treasure

and a treasure it is
for pale like snow
simply isn't the same
as a rich deep tan
or when across a wide, wide range
dandelions fan

and for its likeness, again
the sun gave birth
on a morning both pink & grey
to babies that glowed
and shimmered and shone
flashing in the eye like the first
dawn ray

oh, but they were beautiful!
the Children of the Sun
with illuminous light
kissing their feet
they pranced & skipped
and dazzled with their smiles
and warmed the world with their heat

and then one day
through the gleam of their heat
waddled in a lone, lone child
the golden babies screamed
and recoiled and ran
for the baby was black as night

in the patch of golden
stood now a navy blue
exuding a dark, dark aura
that the Goldens soon named evil,
as they ran out the room

so, it was done
his fate was sealed
his colour, his presence
left room for no deal
stones & leers in his way
fear & disgust bathed his sprit way

his hair black as ebony
his lips cold as snow
the child was no longer small
but a man that was in the wrong

he wondered on his hair
and pondered on his skin
"why is it not golden;
but black & dark unswayed?"

he wept & scratched his flesh
he hid in robes of mesh
so when the beautiful people came
he would agree to their accusations in shame

his head hung lower than ever
the ground was all he dared to see
he would rather look down & hurt himself
than look up & face their swords & spears

the Children of the Sun remained aloof
they weren't guilty, just too gleeful to look
at the man in blue when he was there
and the man in blue when he disappeared

but one day, oh! – the earth then fell
and there was horror everywhere
the golden light that washed them aglow
was moving, never to be seen again

the navy blue took over the sky
and the Children fell down sobbing
"it's the curse of the wretched blue man, for sure!"
yes, but wherever could he be hiding?

a gasp sounded across the crowd
a finger printed towards the dark sky
it was unusual, this, not for the gasp
but for the awe that replaced the horror this time

and one sole girl would notice it then
"aren't those the marks;
the marks on the Blue Man's frame?"
and them the race to his home would start
and the door busted open; quick!
but to no avail, for the Blue Man
was dead and lay there limp

his blood, she'd notice, though, was not red
but a shade of ivory pale
it resembled the shining glitter that was splattered
across his lifeless frame

"good riddance!" said the Goldens & went back home
"he was evil & ugly for sure."
of course, yes!
how could he be pretty?
his hair wasn't shining like gold!

who cares that his teeth were a gleaming white?
who cares that his hair was like molasses?
beauty, remember, is washed in light
it can't be splattered with diamonds priceless!

so what if his eyes were brighter than the sun?
so what if his smile was warm
so what if the same cold child
that the Goldens ignored
would be warmer on the streets
while the blue man froze

so what if his veins shone white?
branches covered in snow through black
it doesn't matter if inside his aura, people felt warm
he wasn't Golden, that was his crime

they say he killed himself, but i disagree
why, he drowned in a sea of hatred,
and loneliness & shame
that killed him & made his fate

and he would never quite know
the extent of his beauty
'cause he was too blind to see
the white, white marks
splattered across his form lean

but when the next morning, the dark began to fade
the Goldens were speechless at
the hues of red & grey

the sight before them now, was never seen before
no shade of golden had ever in a manner so shone

and when the night then came,
and the splatters & the sphere strange appeared
the Children of the Sun, deep in their heart
acknowledged the beauty of the
figures formed in the range

the girl then thought, in bitter, bitter tones
"how sad that the same scenery
is appreciated now when he's dead and bones"
than when he breathed & begged & pleaded
for a little compassion, to which no one heeded
she felt pity for their awestruck faces & exclamations
for they were of late in their realization

the Blue Man covered in white
had to sacrifice life to show them
that his beauty though different
was like the Goldens undefined

and as the clock struck twelve
and the Goldens were washed in silver
the Child of the Night kissed the dark canvas
and ascended to the home where
he'd be welcomed with hugs & smiles

•

it's my life

•

am i some animal?
dumb and lame
or may be a servant
to your words a slave

you fume in anger
& roar & growl
why should i cower
to your hunter-like prowl?

you say you know me
and yet still
my wardrobe is filled
with clothes you bill

"i don't want the damned kurta!"
my heart screams
i want
tops & jeans that are ripped at the seams

i'm not a model daughter
or a perfect doll
but when i drop the act
your accusations are tall

i'm fake, you say
and pretentious
so what are you?
oblivious to my pinch
i'm a badass
a delinquent & a snitch
i stare at crop-tops
and pass by inch

boots, bracelets, spikes and laces
is what i crave
and yet i'm tainted
with ethics & morals & conventions-a-plenty
that with a passion i hate
& would destroy too late

and again one day
you'll walk in angry
scream & shout
and hit me plenty

tears prick, but i glare though It all
am i your servant?
to your words a slave?

you birthed me, not bought me
i'm not your toy
to misdirect anger
and bring to tears

who gave you the right
to make me sad
you're my mother
but such a damn cad
is it my fault your day
went horribly bad?
if you want an excuse
ask nicely, i'll give it, though sad

we're kids
it's our job to be stupid
don't give me shit
if you knew, why'd you do it?

you knew kids weren't a walk in the park
and yet here we are
the villains, by far
you mould us, not our lives
you make us, not our crimes
so, why still, are you trying to control
a jungle tiger
unbeknownst to patrol

A Mini Minstrel's Mind

i'm a free bird
and have my own life
it's not my fate
to be a whiz at math & Science

i'm a sloth, i'm a punk
all the things you don't want
i'm ambitious, i'm great
all the things you're not

i'm not gonna be nice to elders
or be a lady or dress nice
i'm not gonna keep one hand clean
on your dining table tall & neat

in front of company
i'll wear a skirt tight
& short & sparkly
and boots with silver spikes

i'll streak my hair
and wear tube tops
showing off tattoos
on a whim, on a toss

i'll ride bikes
and swear and curse
that's who i am
and i don't remember giving you
the liberty to judge

oh, right! i remember
it's probably cause i didn't
i'm gonna fail everywhere
and shine when i'm there
i'll take your taunts & your hate
when the school is laughing
and throw them back in your face
when with the world, i'll be laughing

yes, i'm average
what're you gonna do about it?
i'm only perfect when the guests
are raving 'what talent she is!'

so who gave you the right?
the right to treat me like shit
what made you think
that you control my things?

you angry?
punch a goddamn pillow, woman,
for a 110
i'm not gonna cry a ton

i don't care what the reason is
and i'm done being understanding
why should i be in despair
while you are so accomplished
and tall and fair?!

i'm not your petty property
i own myself
if it's too much for you to take
go jump in the nearest lake

till 18 you say?
let me make it easy
how about i die today?
so you don't have to pretend
and i don't have to fake
the love & support that's in the wrong direction
as of late

a thousand movies, a thousand books
were made to tell you
before you look

and see a barren, empty land
full of empty promises
and bitterness & sourness

woman, we're a free race
the sky is our home, the clouds at stake
we make our own beauty
and create our own sins
if society don't like it
then society can stuff it

i'm not a puppet
and you don't have the strings
i can be great you know
we don't have to wait for 18

we dream big & fly high
a psychologist, a singer
or a basket player
creating ties

we're delinquents, babe
we make statements
not impressions & grades
or ace those tests

we love with passion
and hate with red
our lives are kaleidoscopes
not a horizon plain in lead

we're insufferable, uncontrollable
inexplicable, irrevocable
we're raw, dark beauty
with scars that bleed
in hues of red and maroons that tweak

we're a splash of colours
a strike of lightning
we're light, we're night
we're a bolt of thunder bright

i know it seems tough,
but, we'll get where's right
have a little faith,
you birthed us, right?

your adjectives to us do their job
we're hurt, we're wounded,
yay, you!
you sadistic lot,

but, you should probably know
that it goes both ways
sure, we could get better
or we could get worse in a day

see, your excuses to yell?
are sort of really lame
you think i'm bad?
oh, baby, i'll show you bad

raise me right is what your job is
so tell me sweet mother
what's right?
prim, proper & tame?

who gets to decide
that burping is rude
i'll burp all i damn want
let's see what you can do

i make my own right
and make my own rules
tsk, tsk, too bad
if you find it rude

i'm your worst nightmare
i'm your evil ghost
i'm a wild beast
grinning & raising a toast

to all of you who think you own me
to all of you who think you can control me
i dare you, try
let's see how far your pry

i'm not here to please you
or to make you fan your face
you and your fancy airs
can shove it for all i care

cause i'm done pretending
and faking and tolerating
you just don't seem to get it
that the king of the jungle?
he's the ruler
your want keep him at home
and make him tame

how dare you yell at me?
how dare you scream
who said your genes had to bring
your model behavior down to me?!

i'm not perfect i'll admit
if anything i'm flawed
extensively, like shit
but, is that your excuse?
to make me cry

and make my day hell
is that your excuse?
to shout for things
that frequent & in all dwells

1 is great
2 is fine
3,4,5,6?
for a moment just stop
and think about it
an entire family can't be wrong
we're like this everywhere
from Delhi to New York

if indulging us is so painful
tell me now
i'll show you how worthless i am
when i earn on my own
cause believe me, i can

take your rules
and goals & regulations
and throw them in the sea
hello, it's me
it's my life, these are my marks
i'll frigging well goddamn top
if i feel like it

i'm done letting you live through me
i'm done with all this shit
its time to make you realize
the girl you knew is dead
i'm only human & i'll change with time
i guess you forgot, though
cause i'm still being treated like child

it's time to show you
show you the light
it's time for you to see the real me
i'm rude, i'm crass
the law lives beneath my ass
i drove on the wrong side of the road before
now i'll redefine illegal & then some more

i'm ill behaved & an embarrassment
i'm society's bitch
i'll smoke & throw back pints
if you don't like it
aw, poor you
i just stopped caring
about your yelling and you

what you think?
just ceased to matter
i don't give a damn
about you & the latter

call me selfish
call me careless
i live for fun
and flip off a dozen

i'm your worst nightmare
i'm your evil ghost
i'm wild beast
grinning and raising a toast

to all of you who think you own me
to all of you who think you can control me
i dare you, try
let's see how far you pry?

…the king of the jungle?
he's the ruler
he lives for the kill
and thrives in the thrill
he has no family
or a cave, or responsibility
it's impossible, you can try but
it simply cannot be done
he'll tear off the leash
and not bother to reach
cause he kills without having moved a tendon

he's free, he's wild
he's different & he's lithe
he's royalty, people
you can't keep him at home
and make him tame

•

the dark knight

•

wave after wave crashes over
drowning me of desperate air
and filling my lungs instead with grief
to which one compares

like a free-fall off a cliff
i am knocked off in horrific measures
like the last leaf of autumn
i fall alone, alone in ordeals,
alone in endeavors

cry no more, child
i wish to tell my eyes
but to whom do i speak?
the mouth of the well is dry

rush, run, oh my knight
i shall fade away soon
forgive me, i speak to the air
my only audience is you, radiant moon

is that pity in your eyes i see?
why, why, my sweet!
avert those soft silver orbs
i'm not worthy of your sympathy

i'm a great vast wasteland
with wild shrubs that grow
i'm the only sorrowful being
who finds beauty in its soul

oh, you heavenly beast, you
such power in your tyranny
you've taken over my mind
at your mercy is my being

perhaps if i were more pliant
and would try to amend
you'd be more complacent
and not bind me to hell

or is it submission you desire?
to straighten up & correct my faults
to lead a productive day
to have a successful life

i know of my faults and the dents-a-plenty
but i'd rather change for me
and not at your expense,

for you, oh demon
are only temporary
child as i am, what shall i do
when you leave to live in glory?

why, i'll be catapulted back
to this strange eerie way
ruthless cruel words
my will don't break, only sway

ssh, though, come hither
i shall whisper my woe in your ear
i let the demon not know
but fall sometimes at the leers

i scramble up quick, hush!
before the devil may notice
notice, though, even if he does
why should a king care for a novice?

my cliff, my sea, my knight, my moon
it hurts not because you say what you say
but more because it's you who utters the word
my love...slowly burning a rune

of despair into my mortal flesh
perish as i wish
but can never achieve

oh, you tragic, fraying bird
are you, too, hurt?
did someone, too, with knives & spears
break your small, weak heart?

and strike hard
before you could recover
from the shock of the venom
tiny, delicate flutter

of wings, lifeless
as you fall to the ground
and heave in a breath
to fill the gaping wound

but, what's this?
you fall short
it reaches your lungs
but not your heart

oh, you heavenly beast, you
such power in you tyranny
words, words creeping slow
look, there lies your trophy

oh, you glorious demon, you
avengeful & bitter
black eyes aglow
you travel alone,
so she unassuming
thought that you must be loved

but, weeks later
here she lies
the sun no longer a guest in her eyes
you had no mortal weapon
she was a foolish creature
your words were your weapon
she refused to realize

never mind, now
go away, you
let her at least die in peace

don't worry, pretty bird
here, the sun comes
he'll take you home & to safety

what's this, oh
you haven't left
i'm certain i told you to go

leave now,
you'll visit soon enough
after all, me too you have to torture

for now though, i think i'll rest
why do you wish to watch me sleep
i beg of you; go away
don't plague & taint my night with nightmares

knight, oh, knight, where are you?
where is your silver sword
you must hurry, valiant soldier
there's little of me left to plunder

and, when you come, if you come
come in softly, & close the door
and stow away your black, black sword
in your equally dark armour

and look, oh, sweet
there i go
the last of me slips away
but worry not
there comes the sun
he'll carry me home & to safety

•

dawn

•

such is your beauty
you rising angel
of warm shades of purple
and of turquoise

dark ebony blue
replaced by shades and hues of woe
as they slowly light
and blend and take flight
colors, colors, bidding their canvas goodbye
"i'll return soon," they whisper
"look for me in the breaks of the morrow."

fluffs of white
replace the splattered glitter of the night
inarticulate and shapeless
like cotton that strewn and littered
across a strange teal sky

and the forest is aglow
black, dark veins branched among green in rows
soft angels dance through them
rustle, hustle, shh
shape after shape lights up
laughing as they twirl with those angels without rest

and from those same clouds
will be heard a delighted giggle
full of innocent, childish glee
fairies, elves, astride whisper
and shower kisses down their home

fall, fall, as well you might,
pure, pristine love settling
and kissing calmly the leaf she sits upon

a swallow here, a sparrow there
who do you talk to, sprightly souls?
is it a friend you address?
embracing and caressing with warmth?
or your beloved?
to whom you'll chirp in shy whispers?

why do you laugh so?
share with me your incentive of happiness
do you now, maybe talk to a passing fairy?
do you now, maybe whisper secrets in her ear,
of whose origin only you shall know?

a shade of green there is not quite so
come tend to it, benefactress
bright, pale, spotless yellow glory
mars and brightens, both, it's rich, green surroundings
kiss it awake, still,
so can it live it's full life, thus
another shade of golden blooms now
on his brother
imparted, fondly, so by the beaming sun above

oh, sweet, sweet dawn
you leave me considering the depth of this life
of my insignificance amongst your bright colours
of your glowing life shining even through death

how do you so bare
such widespread incompetence
to see, and yet not quite
to breathe, yet not so

•

just the way i am

•

i'm not evil
or cruel or sadistic
or oblivious of society or in delusion of being mighty
i'm just own person
oblivious, yes, to my own lonesome

i trust and i hurt
and then cry and coat with rust
but i shrug it off and walk on
like you, like them
a smile i put on

i love and i lose
i decide right, and wrong i choose
i laugh and smile with ease
hiding the sting of pain i feel

i wanna dress weird
i wanna look like a nerd
i want skimpy clothes
and to dance through frost

i want to sing
and feel the music seeping into my bones
i wanna close my eyes
and in a different world or era get lost

i'm not evil
or cruel or sadistic
i'm simply me
plain and realistic

no, i can't study
no, Maths and Science are outta my league
i have a soul, simple and hasty
i have a heart, regardless, dusty
the heart is smiling, the soul is free
both hurt when i'm made to heave

i love you
and it kills me
the disappointment i feel
in your eyes, in your kiss

ask me to write,
and i shall comply
ask me to sing,
and i will try

these are things,
things i love
these are peace
and, for me, all that's above

i have it in me
to show the world
to creep in slowly
or maybe stun in a whirl

this is my journey
this is my life
it's my fate
13 years too late

tattoos and piercings
streaks and fringe
short skimpy clothes
and things that make you cringe

underneath the red,
and what you hate
it's the same baby,
that you once fondly held

a change of clothes,
a change in hair
doesn't change
who smiles and hugs you through tainted rain

let me free
let me be
let me be who i am
without difficulty to breathe

caged and contained
there's little she can do
she can cry, she can sob
she can pull at the chains
that bind her to the room

she'll wither away
a bundle of fire
she'll shake and sway
until her frame begins to sway

there's still time yet
there's still a spark left

unfasten the latch
and watch her fly
as her wings soar

•

acknowledgements

•

This book.

So much effort, so much dedication, so much love has been put into the making of this. Though inconsequential in a world where literary talents are constantly churning out masterpieces; it means the whole world to me to have been able to see this come alive. And while i know well and good that there's a 100% chance that nobody will buy it, and that nobody will even know it exists, or acknowledge its insignificant presence, that's okay. i have felt such unbounded joy, and exhilaration in making this that i acknowledge, love and adore it on behalf of the whole world and then some more.

It's just a bunch of rhyming thoughts, and yet i felt like if there was even a small inkling that i could offer to this beautiful world, i had to do it. i owe it to myself and what little semblance of talent i have.

Where to start? There are simply too many people too thank.

My father, who i am proud to be the daughter of, for relentlessly, tirelessly believing in me, even when i didn't believe in myself. For giving me a sea of chances to redeem myself, or try something new, regardless of past failures. For being so giving, and so forgiving, and completely ignoring all the times i've failed him. He's pure light, with

his cheeky smile and crazy dance moves and
infectious laughter and cheesy wordplay.

My mother, and might i add, my best friend. There are
no words, you unearthly angel. God sent you down
from the moon to grace this world with your beautiful
smile, your enlightening presence, your otherworldly
beliefs and contagious positivity. You have touched
so many lives, made so many existences meaningful
and lightened the world of heavy, heavy burdens, with
every breath you take. i am blessed to have been
given a soul as beautiful as yours as a companion.
i fervently wish to know you in all my lives, whether
as a friend, a sister, or an acquaintance.

My maasi, and my angel's twin, for sitting there
beside me seriously and nodding that cute,
practical, level-headed mind and supporting me,
no matter what, like my own mother would. You
stun me with your power to change this world,
with how silently amazing you are, with your
capability of loving, and your belief in yourself.

My mausa, for sitting there beside me and taking
this book as seriously as a life-changing cars deal. i
don't know what i've done to deserve you caring for
me and loving me enough to sit there beside me and
be so concerned, so bothered, so, so supportive,
but who am i to question my life's only miracle? You
might just decide to change your mind and fly away.

My amazing, brilliant brother, Ansh Srivastava. Thank
you for that sage piece of advice. Never has there

ever been someone with a fire, a light, a brilliance, that has burnt so bright. Whatever this man touches will turn to gold. He has the power to change the world, and i'm not even sure he knows it yet. Thank you for existing, bhai. You make life better. The house lights up and sighs in contentment when you laugh, and your smile has warmth enough to melt steel.

My grandparents, for giving me the most beautiful treasure in the world, my parents, and loving me indirectly through them all because of a family bond, an obligation, because i do realize how little there is to love. Also, a special thanks to my paternal grandmother and literary lover, with whom i've grown up and who has contributed in more than a small way to making this book see the light of the day.

One Farrina Gailey, of Partridge Publishing, who might think of this as stupid, but she will forever be engraved in my mind as the first facet of this beautiful journey she has helped me embark upon.

Another Kathy Lorenzo, for her immeasurable patience in simply doing her job. In her professionalism and finesse, she has made me forever indebted to her.

All the people who let me talk the senseless shit that spouts endlessly from my mouth, and not ignore me or shut me down, granted even, for propriety's sake.

And lastly, you, cherished reader, for picking up this book, and giving it a chance.